BRAND AND LAND

*Your 1-Hour Guide
to Land a 6-Figure Job*

JOHN SIGNO

Copyright © 2023 Signofied, LLC

All rights reserved

No portion of this book may be reproduced in any form without written permission from the publisher or author, except as permitted by U.S. copyright law.

Published by Signofied, LLC

ISBN: 979-8-3912-8572-4

This book is dedicated to all the individuals in the world who found themselves in the job market and have ridden the rollercoaster of emotions. This book is the recipe to landing your new job with new tools and techniques – and a better mindset.

Contents

Foreword 7
Chapter 1: Performance, Identity, and Engagement 11
Chapter 2: Job Search Insights and Tips 15
Chapter 3: Resume 46
Chapter 4: LinkedIn: Your Branding Tool 54
Chapter 5: Understanding Applicant Tracking Systems (ATS) to Optimize your Job Search 64
Chapter 6: Interview 69
Chapter 7: Mindset 78
Conclusion 95
Acknowledgments 97
About the Authors 98

JOHN SIGNO

Foreword

IN TODAY'S HIGHLY competitive job market, standing out from the crowd is more important than ever. With so many talented professionals vying for the same positions, it can be challenging to get noticed by employers. That's where *Brand and Land: Your 1-hour Guide to Land a 6-Figure* Job comes in. This book is designed to help you differentiate yourself from the competition and increase your chances of landing your next opportunity, dream job, or moving up the corporate ladder.

Full disclosure: I have known John Signo since he took my training in 2014. I am the founder and co-owner of BeardedEagle. I function as a Certified Scrum Trainer, Board Certified Coach, Certified Six Sigma Black Belt, and Project Management

Professional in my organization. I have certified tens of thousands of aspiring professionals looking to create a better path for themselves. Many of these professionals get certified and don't know what to do next. Or they are trying to step into a career by grasping at slippery straws.

Many of them still need the secret sauce. Yes, the right skills and strategies matter to navigate this digital landscape. However, how do you do that when you are in the depths of despair? When you have lost your job and no one is calling you back. When no income is coming in, and people depend on you. When unemployment has run out, and you are doing all you can do. I don't understand what that is like, but John does!

Before John landed at Bank of America, this was him. With decades of experience in project management and systems engineering, he worked for some of the most prominent companies in the world, including IBM and J Walter Thompson. This wealth of knowledge did have employers banging on his front door. John picked himself up by his bootstraps to brand himself and create the tools needed to stand out in the crowd.

In this book, John and his Brand and Land team share their strategies and tips for building a brand that gets you noticed by employers. They cover various topics, including creating an ATS bulletproof resume, using LinkedIn to network and showcase your skills, and navigating the online application process. The authors provide practical advice on preparing for interviews, following up after the interview, and negotiating job offers.

I attended the class and read the book. The power and presence of the authors and presenters are captured here. I can guarantee that you can improve your professional reputation by showcasing your unique skills and experience in a way that stands out from other job seekers. They give you practical tips on navigating the online application process, including optimizing your resume and cover letter for the ATS system and tailoring your application to each job posting.

In summary, this book is an excellent resource for anyone who wants to stand out and land their next job. The author's expertise and experience make this book valuable to any job seeker's library. The lessons and insights shared in this book are practical, actionable, and based on real-world experience.

This book is a must-read, whether you are just starting your career or looking for a change. By following their strategies and tips, you will be well on your way to building a personal brand that sets you apart from the competition and helps you land your next job.

Devon Morris
Founder, BeardedEagle

Chapter 1
Performance, Identity, and Engagement

ACHIEVING PERSONAL and career success requires a solid foundation that encompasses a range of different factors. Three essential elements that play a critical role in this process are P.I.E., or Performance, Identity, and Engagement. These three ingredients come together to create a stable foundation that helps individuals progress in their personal and professional lives. In this chapter, we will take a closer look at the importance of P.I.E. in achieving success and how you can work to improve each of these essential ingredients.

Performance

Performance refers to the quality of the work you do, as well as your ability to meet or exceed expectations. It's not just about doing the job but doing it well.

For example, if you're a software developer, your performance is measured by the quality of the code you produce, your ability to meet deadlines, and your overall productivity. Performance is a critical ingredient, but it only accounts for nine percent of P.I.E.

Identity

Identity refers to how you present yourself to others and how you're perceived by them. It encompasses your values, beliefs, and attitudes, as well as the image you project to others. Your identity is your personal brand, and it's important to take ownership of how others perceive you.

A strong identity can help you stand out in a crowded job market or get noticed for a promotion. Identity is the second-most important ingredient, accounting for thirty-one percent of P.I.E.

Engagement

Engagement refers to your ability to connect with others and build meaningful relationships. It encompasses your ability to network, collaborate, and communicate effectively with others.

Engagement is the most critical ingredient, accounting for sixty percent of P.I.E. This is because success in today's world is often determined by whom you know and your ability to form alliances with others.

PIE MODEL

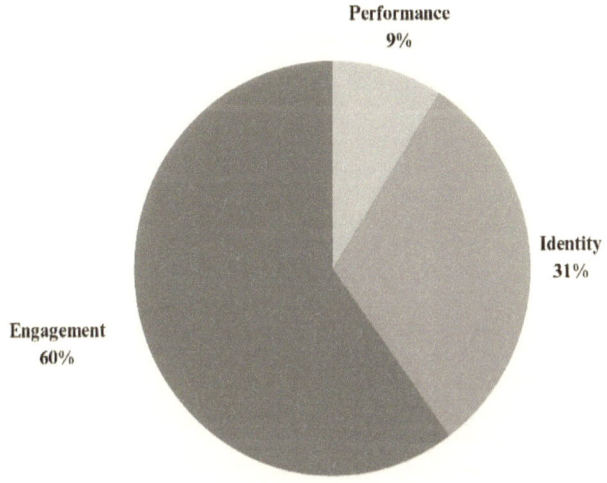

Conclusion

In conclusion, P.I.E. is a powerful recipe for success. It requires a balance of performance, identity, and engagement to create a stable foundation for personal and career growth.

To achieve success, it's important to focus on each of these elements and to continually work to improve them. By doing so, you'll be well on your way to achieving your goals and reaching new heights of success. Remember always to strive to give your best performance, take ownership of your identity, and build meaningful relationships through engagement.

Chapter 2
Job Search Insights and Tips

Welcome to the Job Market!

NAVIGATING
THE JOB SEARCH

Looking For a Job Is Your New Full-time Job

MEET JACK, A thirty-two--year-old male living in San Antonio, Texas. Jack has been unemployed for several months and is now on a mission to find a project management job. He is a highly organized and dedicated individual who is willing to put in the time and effort necessary to achieve his goals.

To increase his chances of success, Jack invested eight hours per day in his job search. He divided his time into two parts, dedicating four hours to posting his resume and cover letter on job boards and other relevant websites. During this time, Jack ensured that each resume was tailored to the specific job he was applying for, highlighting his relevant skills and experiences.

The other four hours of Jack's day were dedicated to learning and networking. He researched companies and industries that interested him, attending networking events and building relationships with recruiters and hiring managers. Jack used his exceptional communication skills to connect with people in his field, establishing a rapport with them and learning more about their organizations.

To stay organized and on top of his job search, Jack used Microsoft OneNote to keep track of his job applications and resumes. This helped him to stay focused and ensure he didn't miss any important deadlines or opportunities.

All of Jack's hard work and dedication paid off when he received a call from a company located in New Braunfels, Texas. They had seen his resume and were impressed by his skills and experience. After several rounds of interviews, Jack was offered a six-figure job as a project manager. He was thrilled to accept the offer and excited to start his new career.

Jack's story is a testament to the power of hard work and dedication. By investing eight hours per day in his job search, he was able to secure a highly desirable position and start a new chapter in his life.

Looking for a job can be a challenging and time-consuming process, but with the right mindset and approach, you can make the most of your job search and find the perfect job.

The first thing to remember is that looking for a job is your new full-time job. Just like our man Jack, you should dedicate eight hours a day to your regular job and invest eight hours a day in your job search. This means setting aside time each day to focus solely on your job search and treating it as you would any other work-related task.

During your eight-hour workday, it's recommended that you dedicate four hours to posting your resume and cover letter on job boards and other relevant websites. This is the time to customize your resume and cover letter for each job application and ensure that you're presenting yourself in the best possible light.

The other four hours of your workday should be dedicated to learning and networking. Use this time to research companies and industries that interest you and learn about the latest trends and developments in your field. Attend networking events, connect with people in your industry, and build relationships with recruiters and hiring managers.

To help manage your job search, it's also a good idea to use tools like OneNote or Excel to keep track of your job applications and resumes. This will help you stay organized and ensure you don't miss any important deadlines or opportunities.

Remember, finding the perfect job takes time, effort, and dedication. By investing eight hours a day in your job search and using the right tools and strategies, you'll be well on your way to landing your dream job. Good luck!

**THE BALANCING ACT
OF JOB SEARCH**

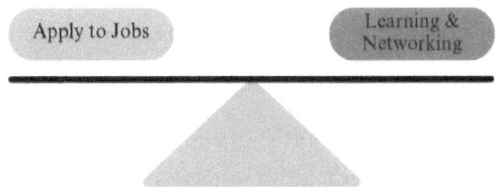

Age Bias Is Alive and Well in The Job Market

Next, you need to think about how to create the "ageless" resume and LinkedIn profile. Because age bias is real, but it can be overcome.

Meet John, a sixty-one-year-old male living in Norfolk, Virginia. John is a highly experienced civil engineer who has worked in the industry for over twenty-five years. Despite his extensive background in naval shipbuilding, John was not getting any calls back from recruiters. He soon realized it was because his resume contained his work experiences from the last twenty-five years, and recruiters were looking for younger candidates.

John struggled to find work for four months and was getting desperate. He called one of his colleagues, who was of a similar age and had recently found employment, for advice. They met for a cup of coffee, and the colleague told John he needed to de-age his resume and include only the last ten years' experience on his resume. John was stunned by the advice and couldn't believe that his age was such a significant factor in his job search. But his colleague explained that this is a job market where youth is served.

John took his colleague's advice and made his resume ageless. He also created a LinkedIn profile that reflected his recent experience and focused on his skills rather than his age. Within one month, John landed a six-figure job at a private sector civil engineering firm in Norfolk, Virginia.

John's new resume and LinkedIn profile highlighted his most recent work experiences and skills, making him a more attractive candidate to recruiters. He was excited to start his new job and grateful for his colleague's advice. John realized that, in today's job market, it's essential to stay current and relevant, regardless of age.

John's story is a reminder that age should not define our value in the workforce. By making his resume ageless and focusing on his most recent experience and skills, John was able to secure a new job in his field. It's a lesson for all job seekers to stay current and relevant and always to adapt to the changing job market.

As we grow older, we often face challenges when it comes to finding new job opportunities. Ageism, or discrimination based on age, is a real and frustrating issue that many job seekers face. However, there are ways to overcome ageism and succeed in your job search.

The first step is to acknowledge that ageism exists and that it may be a factor in your job search. Once you accept this reality, you can take steps to overcome it. Here are some tips to help you fight ageism in the job search process:

1. **Emphasize your skills and experience**. Rather than focusing on your age, highlight your skills and experience. Use your resume and cover letter to showcase the value you can bring to a company.

2. **Keep your skills up to date.** Stay current with the latest technology and industry trends. Take courses or attend workshops to improve your skills and knowledge.

3. **Network.** Networking is key to finding job opportunities, regardless of your age. Attend industry events, and connect with other professionals in your field.

4. **Use social media.** Create a LinkedIn profile and other social media accounts to showcase your skills and experience. Make sure your profile is up to date and relevant to your job search.

5. **Be flexible.** Consider part-time or contract work to get your foot in the door. Be open to new opportunities and willing to adapt to new work environments.

6. **Stay positive.** Don't let ageism discourage you. Keep a positive attitude and stay focused on your goals. Believe in yourself and your abilities.

In fact, millennials and Gen Z also face stereotypes in today's job market; they have to overcome the preconceived notions that they are either too easily distracted or incompetent in today's workforce. By focusing on your relevant skills and experience, you can demonstrate that you are a valuable asset to the company, regardless of your age.

Remember, ageism is a challenge that many job seekers face, but it doesn't have to hold you back. By emphasizing your skills and experience, staying current with industry trends, networking, using social media, being flexible, and staying positive, you can overcome ageism and find success in your job search.

Interview Process Has Evolved but Preparation Remains the Same

Meet Lily, a thirty-four-year-old business analyst living in Seattle, Washington. Lily was excited to interview for a virtual job position with a panel of interviewers. She dressed casually in her comfortable yoga dress for the interview, not realizing how important her attire could be in creating a professional impression. Unfortunately, this casual approach led to her losing the job, as the employer didn't take her seriously.

Feeling dejected, Lily confided in her network of girlfriends about her situation while they were out shopping and having lunch. Her best friend, Samantha, who worked in HR, explained that companies were looking for job seekers who were professionally dressed, whether they were interviewing in-person or virtually.

The next business analyst role that came up, Lily didn't waste any time looking her professional best. She selected a smart and stylish business suit, tasteful accessories, and polished shoes to give herself an extra edge. She practiced her interview skills, researched the company, and prepared thoroughly for the interview.

As it turned out, Lily's professional attire and preparedness paid off. She was offered the job and began her new role with enthusiasm. Lily made her mark in the new company and quickly proved herself to be an asset. Thanks to her hard work, dedication, and professional attitude, Lily was recognized with a 5-star award for her outstanding performance in her role.

Through her experience, Lily learned that dressing professionally is not just about making a good impression on an employer, but it is also a reflection of your attitude, confidence, and preparedness. Whether you're interviewing for a job in person or virtually, it's important to always dress professionally and present yourself in the best possible light.

The job interview process has certainly evolved over the years. With the rise of technology, virtual interviews have become more common, and with the ongoing pandemic, they have become the norm. However, even as the process has changed, the importance of preparation has not.

One crucial aspect of preparation for any interview is dressing professionally. It's important to understand that dressing professionally for virtual interviews is just as important as it is for in-person interviews. Even though you may not be meeting the interviewer face-to-face, you still want to create a good impression and show that you take the process seriously.

When dressing for a virtual interview, make sure to dress professionally from head to toe. You never know when you might need to stand up or move around, and you don't want to be caught off guard. Choose a professional outfit that is appropriate for the job and industry you are applying for. Avoid wearing anything too distracting or revealing, and make sure your clothes are clean and pressed.

For in-person interviews, dressing professionally is even more critical. You want to make a good impression from the moment you walk into the building. Dress in business professional attire, including a suit or dress pants and blouse, and make sure your hair and makeup are neat and polished. If you're not sure what to wear, do some research on the company's dress code and dress a level up from that.

Consistency is also essential in your appearance. If you wear glasses or contacts, make sure to wear them to the interview. Avoid any sudden hairstyle changes or drastic makeup looks. You want the interviewer to focus on your qualifications and experience, not on your appearance.

Finally, it's crucial to show respect for the job interview process. This means being punctual, turning off your cell phone or any other distractions, and treating everyone you encounter with kindness and respect. Remember, the interviewer is evaluating not only your qualifications but also your professionalism and interpersonal skills.

In conclusion, while the job interview process may have evolved with the rise of virtual interviews, the importance of dressing professionally and preparing for the interview has not changed. Whether it's a virtual or in-person interview, make sure to dress appropriately, be consistent, and show respect for the process to make the best impression possible.

INTERVIEW SESSION

One crucial aspect of preparation for any interview is dressing professionally.

Buy Health Insurance and Manage Your Expenditures During Your Job Search

Meet our protagonist, Jane, a forty-six-year-old single mother of twin teenagers living in Little Rock, Arkansas. She has been struggling to make ends meet, juggling various part-time jobs to pay for rent, groceries, and utilities. She has been applying for HR generalist roles, hoping to secure a steady income and better benefits for her family.

Despite her efforts to make a decent living, Jane had not purchased health insurance, as she couldn't afford the premiums. Unfortunately, her son, who had a pre-existing condition, had a medical emergency and was admitted to the ER. After his discharge, Jane was shocked to receive a bill of $35,000 for the hospital visit, and she didn't know how to afford it. With other past-due bills piling up, she was stressed out and felt like she was drowning in debt.

Determined to provide for her family, Jane continued her job search while trying to figure out a way to manage the mounting bills. After several interviews and rejections, Jane finally landed an HR generalist role at a local company. She was relieved to finally have a steady income and better benefits, including health insurance coverage for her family.

Jane learned the hard way about the importance of health insurance and budget management during her job search. She realized that securing a stable job and financial stability was not easy, and she had to make difficult decisions and sacrifices to provide for her family. Nevertheless, Jane's perseverance and resilience paid off, and she was able to overcome the odds and improve her family's situation.

In the end, Jane's story serves as a reminder that, despite the challenges and setbacks, there is always hope and a way forward for those who are determined and willing to work hard.

Finding a job can be a stressful and challenging experience, but it can become even more daunting when you don't have health insurance. Without insurance, even a minor illness or injury can lead to substantial medical bills, which can add to the stress of job searching. Fortunately, there are several ways to obtain health insurance during a job search.

Firstly, if you were previously employed and had health insurance through your employer, you may be eligible for COBRA continuation coverage. COBRA allows you to keep your health insurance for a limited time after leaving your job, although you will be responsible for paying the full cost of the premium. This can be expensive, but it may be a good option if you have a pre-existing condition that would make it difficult to obtain insurance through other means.

Secondly, you may be eligible for Medicaid or the Children's Health Insurance Program (CHIP). These programs provide free or low-cost health insurance to low-income individuals and families. Eligibility varies by state, so it's important to check your state's requirements.

Another option is to purchase health insurance through the Health Insurance Marketplace. The Marketplace offers plans with different levels of coverage and costs, and you may be eligible for subsidies based on your income. You can apply online or by phone, and open enrollment occurs during specific periods of the year.

Lastly, some professional organizations or unions offer health insurance to their members. This may be a good option if you are part of a professional organization or union, or if you plan to join one.

In conclusion, obtaining health insurance during a job search can be challenging, but there are several options available. COBRA continuation coverage, Medicaid/CHIP, the Health Insurance Marketplace, and professional organizations or unions are all potential sources of health insurance coverage. It's important to research your options, understand your eligibility, and consider your budget when selecting a plan. Having health insurance can provide peace of mind during a job search and protect you from unexpected medical bills.

Manage Your Emotions

Managing your emotions during a job search and interview is crucial to your success in finding the right job. Job searching can be stressful, and interviews can be nerve-wracking, but if you can manage your emotions effectively, you can increase your chances of getting hired. Here are some tips for managing your emotions during a job search and interview:

1. **Practice mindfulness:** Mindfulness is an excellent tool for managing anxiety, anger, and depression during a job search. Take a few minutes each day to practice mindfulness techniques like deep breathing, meditation, or yoga. This can help you stay calm, centered, and focused during the job search process.

2. **Recognize and label your emotions:** If you're feeling anxious, angry, or depressed during a job search, it's important to recognize and label these emotions. Labeling your emotions can help you better understand what you're feeling and why. This can help you manage your emotions more effectively and avoid reacting impulsively.

3. **Use positive self-talk:** Positive self-talk can be a powerful tool for managing emotions during a job search. Instead of focusing on

negative thoughts or self-doubt, try to focus on positive affirmations. Repeat positive statements to yourself like "I am capable and confident" or "I am worthy of success" throughout the job search process.

Example 1: Sarah is a recent college graduate looking for her first job. She's struggling with anxiety and self-doubt, which is making it difficult for her to interview well. Sarah starts practicing mindfulness and deep breathing techniques, which helps her manage her anxiety. She also starts using positive self-talk and focusing on her strengths and accomplishments. With practice, Sarah becomes more confident and lands a job that she loves.

Example 2: Michael is a middle-aged man who recently lost his job. He's struggling with depression and anger, which is affecting his job search. Michael starts practicing mindfulness and cognitive-behavioral therapy, which helps him manage his depression and anger. He also starts working on recognizing and labeling his emotions, which helps him avoid reacting impulsively. With practice, realized he couldn't do this alone and needed all the help he could get.

With the support of his loved ones, John started to feel more confident and motivated in his job search. He reached out to his old mentors and networked with new people in the industry. He also learned about the importance of health insurance coverage and managing a household budget during a job search the hard way.

Finally, after months of searching, John landed a job as an account manager. He was overjoyed and grateful to his family, friends, and mentors who supported him throughout the journey.

In conclusion, John learned the hard way that asking for help is not a sign of weakness. It takes courage to admit you need help and to ask for it. By lowering his pride and speaking to his family, friends, and mentors about his job search, John was able to find a job and provide for his family. He also learned valuable lessons about health insurance coverage and managing a household budget during a job search, which he would carry with him for the rest of his life.

When it comes to job searching, connecting with local recruiters can be a game-changer. Not only can they provide valuable insights into the job market and potential opportunities, but they can also serve as advocates for you during the hiring process. Here are some tips on how to connect with local recruiters and maximize your chances of finding your dream job:

1. **Schedule coffee appointments with them:** Networking with recruiters can be as simple as setting up a coffee appointment with them. Use online scheduling tools like Calendly, Google, or Outlook to make the process easy and convenient for both parties. This will give you an opportunity to build a personal relationship with the recruiter and learn more about potential job openings.

2. **Share your motivation and willingness**: When you meet with a recruiter and/or hiring manager, make sure to highlight your motivation for finding a new job and your willingness to learn new skills. This will show the recruiter that you are committed to your

job search and willing to put in the effort to succeed. It may also help you stand out from other candidates who are not as proactive in their job search.

3. **Sign an RTR**: An RTR is a Right to Represent, one job per recruiter. If a recruiter presents you with a job opportunity, be sure to sign a Right to Represent (RTR) agreement. This agreement ensures that the recruiter is the only one representing you for that particular job and helps avoid conflicts or misunderstandings. It is important to remember that each recruiter should only represent you for one job at a time.

4. **Build a consistent and professional brand on social media**: Finally, make sure to build a consistent and professional brand on social media platforms like TikTok, Instagram, ClubHouse, and LinkedIn. These platforms provide a great opportunity to showcase your skills, accomplishments, and professional interests. Make sure your profile is up to date and includes relevant information that can

catch the attention of recruiters and potential employers. Additionally, engage with industry leaders and recruiters on these platforms to build your network and increase your visibility.

By following these tips, you can successfully connect with local recruiters and increase your chances of finding your dream job. Remember to always be professional, proactive, and open to learning new skills. Good luck!

10 Websites to Learn a New High-Paying Skill

- www.Udemy.com
- www.Coursera.org
- www.EDX.org
- www.Codecademy.com
- www.SkillCrush.com
- www.Skillshare.com
- www.LinkedIn.com/Learning
- www.Udacity.com

- www.Coursica.com
- TeamTreehouse.com

Online Job Search Resources

Mobile Apps (iOS and Android)

- Glassdoor (also provides salary information)
- Dice Careers
- Indeed
- ZipRecruiter

WIOA (Workforce Innovation Opportunity Act)

The Workforce Innovation and Opportunity Act (WIOA) is a federal law that aims to help individuals who are unemployed or underemployed find better job opportunities. If you're struggling to find work, WIOA can provide you with the resources and support you need to get back on your feet.

One of the key benefits of WIOA is that it provides access to job training and education programs. These programs can help you learn new skills that are in high demand in your local job market, making you a more competitive candidate for open positions.

To take advantage of WIOA, you'll need to visit your local American Job Center. These centers provide a range of services to job seekers, including career counseling, job placement assistance, and access to training programs. The staff at the job center can help you determine if you're eligible for WIOA services and connect you with the resources you need to succeed.

In addition to training and education programs, WIOA also offers financial assistance to eligible job seekers. This assistance can include things like transportation vouchers, childcare support, and funding to help cover the costs of training programs.

To make the most of WIOA, it's important to be proactive in your job search. Take advantage of the resources available to you, attend job fairs and networking events, and stay up to date on the latest job openings in your field. With the right mindset and the support of WIOA, you can take control of your job search and find the career path that's right for you.

Knowledge and Certifications

Acquiring knowledge and certifications is a crucial step for career growth. It helps individuals gain practical knowledge and become more valuable in their field. However, it is important to have a clear understanding of your end goal and research what you need to know and what certifications are worthwhile. Rushing through the process can be detrimental and result in missed opportunities.

Tips for acquiring knowledge and certifications:

1. Understand your end goal and research what you need to know and what certifications are worthwhile.

2. Don't chase or rush certifications. Understand the materials, and apply it into practical knowledge. Take your time, and understand the foundational knowledge that will be crucial in your role.

3. Make it logical. Jumping to the harder certifications will mean you miss out on important foundational knowledge, which is crucial for a lot of roles.

4. There is a chance of failure, so be prepared to learn from it. Don't give up, try again, and take it as an opportunity to learn.

Meet Frank, a software engineer who had been working in the same company for over ten years. He realized he had been stagnant in his career and wanted to make a change. He researched and decided he wanted to become a project manager in the tech industry.

Frank started with the foundational certifications and earned his Certified Scrum Master (CSM), Certified Scrum Product Owner (CSPO), and Scaled Agile Framework (SAFe) certifications. These certifications helped him gain practical knowledge and understand the principles of agile project management.

Frank didn't rush into the next certification; he made it logical and worked on gaining experience as a project manager. He gained valuable experience and learned from his mistakes.

After gaining enough experience, Frank decided to go for the Project Management Professional (PMP) certification. He studied hard, failed the first time, but learned from his mistakes and passed the second time. The certification gave him the validation and recognition he needed to apply for project management positions.

Frank applied for a project management position in a tech company and landed the job. His certifications and experience helped him stand out among the other candidates.

Acquiring knowledge and certifications takes time and effort, but it is worth it in the long run. It helps individuals gain practical knowledge and become more valuable in their field. Understanding your end goal and taking the time to research what you need to know is crucial. Don't rush into certifications, and be prepared to learn from failure.

Chapter 3
Resume

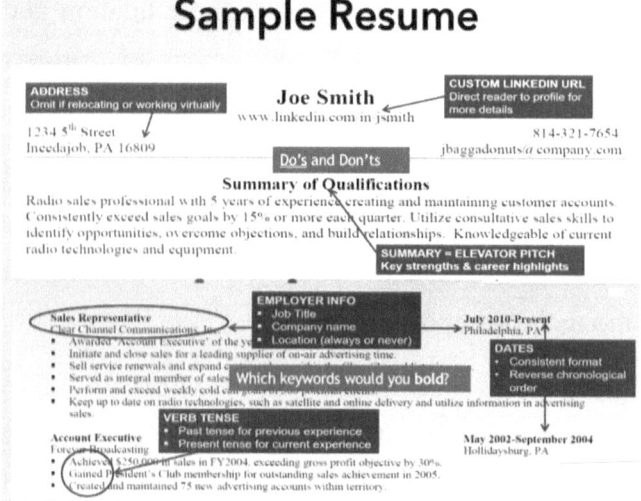

Emily's Story

EMILY SAT AT HER desk, staring at the computer screen in front of her. She had been studying her resume for hours now, making small tweaks and changes, trying to get it just right. She had been searching for a new job for months, and despite having years of experience and a good education, she had yet to find the right fit.

She took a deep breath and scrolled down to the bottom of the page. There, in small font, was the date of her graduation from college. She remembered reading somewhere that it was best to remove the graduation year from your resume, if you had been out of school for a while. It made you seem older and potentially less desirable to some employers.

Emily quickly removed the graduation year and saved the file. She then renamed it, following the new format she had learned: "Emily Smith-ABC Company-Marketing Manager Resume.docx." She made sure to keep it under two pages and used a 12-point font size. She also made sure to highlight her strengths from Strengths Finders.

Feeling satisfied with her changes, Emily decided to take a break and grab a cup of coffee. As she walked to the kitchen, she thought about the other resume tips she had learned. She had started using

OneNote to manage her resumes for job postings, and she always emailed herself a copy for easy access. She had also stopped posting her resume on LinkedIn and started using a cloud service for safe storage.

As she sipped her coffee, Emily thought about the do's and don'ts she had learned. She made sure to use dashes instead of bullet points, and she avoided using headers and footers or tables, since ATS might not read the content inside. She also made sure to avoid full-page lines and providing her full home address, to avoid identity theft. Finally, she always proofread her resume to ensure it was free of errors.

Emily sat back down at her desk and started to make bold the keywords in her resume. She strategically placed them to grab the reader's attention and used keywords found in the job description. She knew this would help her resume get past the ATS and be noticed by recruiters.

Emily looked at her resume one last time, feeling proud of the changes she had made. She had followed the SIGNOFIED principles: it was simple, individualized, got to the point, covered no more than the past ten years, focused on objectives and key results, was factual, intentionally keyword-focused, and delivered exceptional value.

Feeling confident, Emily hit the submit button on a job application she had been eyeing for weeks. She then sat back and waited, hoping her resume would catch the attention of the hiring manager.

Days went by, and Emily started to lose hope. She had applied for so many jobs with no response. She wondered if there was something wrong with her resume or if there were simply too many qualified applicants. She started to feel discouraged and wondered if she would ever find the right job.

One day, as Emily was scrolling through her emails, she saw a message from a recruiter. They had found her resume online and were interested in discussing a job opportunity with her. Emily was shocked and excited. Finally, her hard work had paid off.

Over the next few weeks, Emily went through a series of interviews, all of which went well. She felt like she had finally found the perfect fit. She used her resume as a guide, highlighting her strengths and using the keywords she had learned. Finally, she got the call she had been waiting for: the job was hers.

Emily started her new job feeling confident and proud. She had learned so much about creating an ageless resume and had followed all the tips and tricks she had learned. She knew she had the right skills and experience, and her resume had helped earn the right to win the interview and job.

Resume Tips

The job search process can be overwhelming, but your resume is your ticket to landing your dream job. A well-crafted resume can set you apart from the competition and get you noticed by potential employers. In this guide, we will provide you with essential tips and strategies to create a resume that is ageless, concise, and keyword focused.

Ageless Resume

Your resume should showcase your skills and experience, not your age. To create an ageless resume, limit your work experience to the past ten years, and remove graduation year(s) from your education section.

Additionally, rename the file as "Your Name-Company Name-Job Title Resume.docx," use a 12-point font size, and highlight your strengths using Strengths Finders. Use OneNote or Excel to manage multiple resumes for different job postings and email a copy to yourself for safekeeping. Avoid posting your resume on LinkedIn; instead, store it on a cloud service for easy access.

Do's and Don'ts

Your resume should be easy to read, printable, and free of errors. Use dashes instead of bullet points, type in 12-point font, and avoid using headers and footers or tables.

Do not include full-page lines, and only provide your location as "New York" or "Los Angeles Metro." If you are working from home or remotely, omit your location.

Also, avoid providing your full home address to prevent identity theft, and always proofread your resume for spelling errors, typos, and grammatical mistakes.

Bolding Keywords in Your Resume

Bolding keywords in your resume will help grab the reader's attention and increase your chances of being selected for an interview. Use keywords found in the job description, and place them strategically throughout your resume.

Is Your Resume SIGNOFIED?

Your resume should be SIGNOFIED, meaning it should be:

- Simple
- Individualized
- Gets to the point (concise)
- No more than past ten years (relevant)
- Factual
- Intentionally keyword-focused
- Exposure to networks and recruiters
- Deliver exceptional value

A well-crafted resume is an essential tool in your job search arsenal. By following the tips and strategies outlined in this guide, you can create a resume that is ageless, concise, and keyword-focused, increasing your chances of landing your dream job.

Remember to keep your resume updated and to tailor it for each job application. Good luck!

Chapter 4
LinkedIn: Your Branding Tool

1. SEO Header

THE LINKEDIN SEO header is the section at the top of your LinkedIn profile that includes your name, headline, and profile picture. This section is crucial for getting noticed by potential employers and recruiters, as it is often the first thing they see when they search for candidates on LinkedIn.

By optimizing your LinkedIn SEO header with relevant keywords, a clear and concise headline, and a professional profile picture, you can increase your visibility and attract more attention from recruiters and hiring managers. Additionally, a well-crafted LinkedIn SEO header can help establish your personal brand and differentiate you from other candidates, which can be especially important in competitive job markets.

Overall, paying attention to your LinkedIn SEO header and making sure it is optimized for search can be a key factor in your job search success.

Tips:

- Keep it under 150 characters.
- Captivate the viewer.
- Remove any current/past employer from SEO header.

2. ABOUT Section

The About section on LinkedIn is an opportunity to provide a brief summary of who you are, your professional background, and your goals. It is an important section to leverage for job search, because it provides an opportunity to showcase your personality, your skills, and your professional values to potential employers and recruiters.

To make the most of the About section, focus on crafting a concise and compelling summary that highlights your unique strengths and experiences, as well as your career aspirations. It is also a good idea to include relevant keywords that align with your career goals. Tailor the content of your About section to the job or industry you are targeting.

A well-crafted About section can help you stand out from other candidates and increase your chances of getting noticed by potential employers.

Tips:
- Tell your story.
- Include your contact information.

- As the last line, post the date stamp of past update.

3. Experience

The Experience section on LinkedIn is a critical component of your profile, as it showcases your professional history and expertise. To leverage this section for job search, it is essential to create a detailed and comprehensive record of your work experience, including job titles, responsibilities, and achievements.

It is also important to use relevant keywords and phrases to highlight your skills and accomplishments, which can make it easier for potential employers to find you through LinkedIn's search algorithm. To stand out from other candidates, consider adding multimedia content, such as videos or slideshows, to showcase your work or projects.

Finally, make sure your experience section is up to date and reflects your most recent work experiences, which can demonstrate your industry knowledge and expertise to potential employers.

Tips:

- Don't age yourself: leave education years out.
- Avoid these bullets (see image below) and use dashes instead:

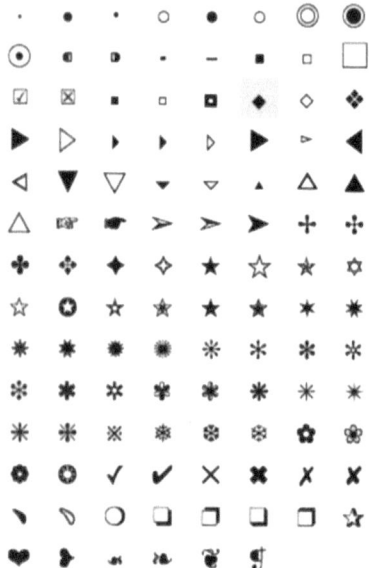

4. Skills and Endorsements

The Skills and Endorsement section on LinkedIn is an opportunity to showcase your areas of expertise and to receive endorsements from other LinkedIn users.

To leverage this section for job search, it is important to carefully choose and list your most relevant skills, ensuring that they align with the job or industry you are targeting.

You can also increase the visibility of your skills by asking your connections to endorse you or endorse them in return. Endorsements can add credibility to your skills and provide social proof of your abilities to potential employers.

Additionally, you can improve your chances of being found in search results by including relevant keywords in your skills section. Finally, make sure to keep your skills section up to date and relevant, and remove any outdated or irrelevant skills.

Overall, the Skills and Endorsement section is a valuable tool for job seekers looking to highlight their expertise and stand out from the competition.

Tips:
- Ask your network to endorse you.
- Add your hard/soft skills.

5. Recommendations

The Recommendations section on LinkedIn is a powerful tool that allows others to publicly endorse your skills and abilities. To leverage this section for job search, it is important to proactively request recommendations from colleagues, managers, and clients who can speak to your strengths and work ethic.

A well-written recommendation can provide social proof of your capabilities and add credibility to your profile. It is also a good idea to strategically choose the right people to ask for recommendations, based on their expertise, position, or their relationship to the industry or job you are targeting.

When requesting a recommendation, provide clear guidance on the type of recommendation you are seeking, and be specific about the skills or qualities you would like to highlight. Finally, make sure to reciprocate by writing recommendations for others, which can build your network and increase the likelihood of receiving recommendations in return.

Tips:

- Have at least two within the last two years

6. Generating a LinkedIn CV/Resume

Generating a LinkedIn resume, or "resume builder," can be a valuable tool for job seekers looking to streamline their job search. By using the information already available on your LinkedIn profile, such as your work experience, education, and skills, you can quickly create a professional-looking resume that can be tailored to fit specific job applications. This can save you time and effort, especially if you are applying to multiple jobs.

Additionally, using a LinkedIn resume can also help ensure that your resume is up to date and consistent with your online profile, which can boost your credibility with potential employers.

Overall, using a LinkedIn resume builder can be a smart and effective way to enhance your job search efforts and stand out from the competition. Moreover, generating a LinkedIn resume can be particularly useful for those using the LinkedIn Easy

Apply feature to apply for jobs directly through the platform.

Tutorial:
- Go to your LinkedIn profile.
- Click on "More" and then click "Save to PDF."

Vanity URL

Using a vanity URL for your LinkedIn profile can be a simple but effective way to brand yourself and make your profile more professional.

A vanity URL is a customized web address that replaces the long, complex URL assigned by LinkedIn by default. By creating a vanity URL that includes your name or some variation of it, you can make it easier for people to find you online and ensure that your LinkedIn profile appears higher in search engine results.

Including your LinkedIn vanity URL on your resume can be a great way to make a positive impression on potential employers and showcase your professionalism. By providing a clear, easy-to-remember link to your LinkedIn profile in your resume, you can demonstrate your commitment to building a strong online presence and highlight your relevant skills and experience in a way that complements your resume.

Tutorial

- Navigate to your LinkedIn profile.

- In the upper right corner, click *"Edit public profile & URL tab."*

- In the upper right corner, click *"Edit your custom URL."*

- Click on the blue-colored pencil icon, and remove the randomly assigned numbers and letters.

- Enter your customized URL name:

  linkedin.com/in/firstname-lastname

Chapter 5

Understanding Applicant Tracking Systems (ATS) to Optimize your Job Search

Introduction

THE JOB APPLICATION process has changed significantly over the years, with technology playing an increasingly critical role in connecting job seekers with potential employers. One of the most significant technological advancements in this area is the Applicant Tracking System (ATS), which has revolutionized the way companies filter and assess job applications.

In this chapter, we will explain how the ATS works and provide two illustrations to help you visualize the process. By understanding the ATS, you will be better equipped to optimize your job search and increase your chances of landing the job you want.

How the ATS Works

The Applicant Tracking System streamlines the recruitment process for companies by automating the initial screening of resumes. Here's a step-by-step breakdown of how the ATS works:

1. **Apply through a company website or another platform.** Job seekers submit their resumes through a company's website, job boards, or other online platforms. These platforms are often integrated with the company's ATS, ensuring that all submitted applications are sent directly to the system for processing.

2. **The resume provided runs through a parsing software.** Once a resume is received, the ATS uses a parsing software to extract relevant information from the document. This software is designed to identify and

categorize details, such as your name, contact information, work history, education, and skills.

3. **The parsing software categorizes based on content, ID, and keywords entered by the hiring manager.** After parsing the resume, the ATS organizes the information based on predetermined categories, such as work experience, education, and skills. Hiring managers can also enter specific keywords related to the job posting, allowing the system to scan for these terms within each resume.

4. **The resume is then assigned a relevancy score based on the keywords and qualifications for the position.** The ATS assigns a relevancy score to each resume based on how closely the content matches the job posting's requirements. Factors that contribute to this score include the presence of relevant keywords, the applicant's years of experience, and their level of education.

5. **The recruiter reviews the resumes that meet a score threshold of at least 75%.** To streamline the process for recruiters, the ATS filters out resumes that fall below a certain relevancy score threshold (typically around seventy-five percent). This allows recruiters to focus on the most promising candidates and reduce the time spent reviewing unqualified applications.

THE ATS WORKFLOW

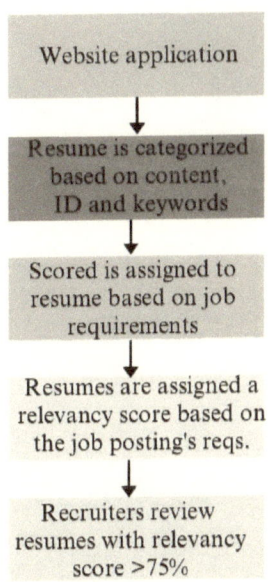

Conclusion

Understanding how the Applicant Tracking System works is crucial for job seekers who want to improve their chances of landing their desired job. By tailoring your resume to include relevant keywords and qualifications, you can optimize your application to score higher in the ATS and increase the likelihood that a recruiter will review your resume and schedule an interview.

Chapter 6
Interview

INTERVIEWING FOR A JOB can be nerve-wracking, especially if it's your first time or if you're transitioning to a new career. However, with the right preparation, you can ace the interview and land the job you want.

In this chapter, we'll discuss some essential tips to help you prepare for your interview, including dress code, body language, elevator speeches, STAR stories, salary negotiation, and the power of the thank-you letter.

1. Dress Code

Dressing appropriately for an interview is crucial. Your appearance can influence the interviewer's first impression of you. Here are some tips to help you dress for success:

- **Research the company's dress code.** Some companies have a formal dress code, while others have a more casual one. You can usually find this information on the company's website or by asking the recruiter or HR representative.

- **Dress conservatively.** Even if the company has a casual dress code, it's still best to dress conservatively for an interview. A suit and tie or a dress and blazer are always safe choices. Remember: You can always "dress-down" (e.g., remove a tie/blazer), but you can't add a tie/blazer during the interview.

- **Make sure your clothes are clean and pressed.** Wrinkled or dirty clothes can give the impression that you're not serious about the interview.

- **Wear comfortable shoes.** You may be asked to walk around the office or go on a tour, so make sure your shoes are comfortable and appropriate for the occasion.

- **Keep jewelry and accessories to a minimum.** Simple jewelry and accessories are fine, but too much can be distracting.

2. Body Language

Body language is another important aspect of your interview. Your body language can convey confidence, enthusiasm, and engagement. Here are some tips to help you make a positive impression:

- **Maintain eye contact.** This shows that you're engaged and interested in the conversation.

- **Sit up straight.** Slouching can give the impression that you're not interested or lack confidence.

- **Smile.** A genuine smile can put the interviewer at ease and make you appear more approachable.

- **Avoid fidgeting.** Fidgeting can be distracting and give the impression that you're nervous or not focused.

- **Use hand gestures.** Appropriate hand gestures can emphasize your points and make you appear more enthusiastic.

3. Elevator Speeches

An elevator speech is a brief introduction about yourself, your skills, and what you bring to the table. It's called an elevator speech because you should be able to deliver it in the time it takes to ride an elevator with someone.

Here are some tips to help you prepare:

- **Be concise.** Your elevator speech should be no longer than thirty seconds to a minute.

- **Focus on your unique selling points.** Highlight your skills, experience, and achievements that make you stand out from other candidates.

- **Tailor your speech to the job you're applying for.** Make sure your speech emphasizes the skills and experience that are most relevant to the position.

- **Practice your speech.** Practice your speech in front of a mirror or with a friend to make sure it sounds natural and confident.

4. STAR Stories

STAR stands for **S**ituation, **T**ask, **A**ction, and **R**esult. These stories are used to showcase your skills and abilities by providing specific examples of when you demonstrated them.

Use the STAR format when answering behavioral interview questions. Here's how to use the STAR format:

- **Situation**: Describe the situation you were in.
- **Task**: Describe the task or challenge you faced.
- **Action**: Describe the action you took to overcome the challenge.
- **Result**: Describe the result of your action.

Here are some tips to help you prepare your STAR stories:

- **Think about your experiences.** Identify experiences in your past jobs or personal life that showcase your skills and abilities.

- **Choose relevant experiences.** Choose experiences that are relevant to the position you're applying for.

- **Practice.**

5. Salary Negotiation

Salary negotiation can be intimidating, but it's an important part of the interview process. Here are some tips to help you negotiate your salary:

- **Do your research.** Research the industry standard for the position and location you're applying for. Websites like Glassdoor and PayScale can help you find this information.

- **Know your worth.** Consider your experience, skills, and education when determining your worth. Make sure you're not undervaluing yourself.

- **Wait for the employer to bring up salary.** It's best to wait for the employer to bring up salary during the interview process. If they ask about your salary expectations, provide a range rather than a specific number.

- **Be confident**. When negotiating, be confident and assertive but also respectful. Remember, negotiation is a discussion, not a confrontation.

- **Consider other benefits**. If the employer isn't able to meet your salary expectations, consider other benefits such as flexible work arrangements, additional vacation time, or professional development opportunities.

6. The Power of the Thank-You Letter

A thank-you letter is a great way to show appreciation and reiterate your interest in the position after the interview. Here are some tips to help you write a powerful thank you letter:

- **Send the letter promptly.** Send the thank-you letter within twenty-four hours of the interview to show your enthusiasm and professionalism.

- **Address the interviewer by name.** Address the interviewer by name, and thank them for their time and consideration.

- **Reiterate your interest.** Use the letter to reiterate your interest in the position and why you're a good fit.

- **Personalize the letter.** If possible, personalize the letter by referencing specific points from the interview or something you learned about the company.

- **Proofread the letter.** Make sure to proofread the letter for any errors before sending it.

Conclusion

Preparing for an interview can be a daunting task, but with the right preparation, you can succeed. Remember to dress appropriately, use positive body language, prepare your elevator speech, and STAR stories, negotiate your salary, and send a thank you letter after the interview.

By following these tips, you can make a great impression and increase your chances of landing the job you want. Good luck!

# Chapter 7
Mindset

The Importance of a Positive Mindset in the Job Search

WELCOME TO THE NEW job market! The job search can be a challenging and stressful process, especially if it takes longer than expected to find the right opportunity. However, maintaining a positive mental attitude can make all the difference in your search.

A positive mindset can help you stay motivated, focused, and resilient throughout the job search journey. In this chapter, we'll explore strategies for maintaining a positive mental attitude during the job search process.

Understand the Power of a Positive Mindset

Research has shown that having a positive attitude can have a significant impact on job search success. When you maintain a positive mindset, you're more likely to approach your job search with a clear head, make better decisions, and be more resilient in the face of setbacks.

Surround Yourself with Positivity

Surround yourself with positive people who support you and believe in your abilities. Seek out mentors or colleagues who can provide you with guidance and support during your job search as they may even have opportunities in store for you.

Having a strong support system can help you stay motivated and optimistic throughout your search.

Focus on Your Strengths

It's easy to get caught up in your weaknesses or past mistakes during the job search process. However, focusing on your strengths and what you have to offer can help you stay positive and confident.

Make a list of your skills, achievements, and unique qualities, and review it regularly to remind yourself of your value. This may even serve as transferrable skills when pivoting in the job search journey.

Stay Organized

Staying organized during your job search can help reduce stress and increase your productivity. Use a job search tracking tool or spreadsheet to keep track of your applications, interviews, and follow-up tasks.

Knowing that you're on top of your job search can help you feel more in control and positive about your progress.

Practice Self-Care

Self-care is critical for maintaining a positive mindset during the job search process. Do things that make you happy and help you relax, such as taking a bubble bath, reading a book, or practicing mindfulness.

Prioritizing self-care can help you stay calm, focused, and positive.

Celebrate Small Wins

It's easy to get caught up in the big picture during the job search process, but celebrating small wins can help you stay positive and motivated.

Celebrate each application submitted, each interview attended, and each positive feedback received. These small wins can help you stay on track and maintain a positive outlook.

Stay Connected

Networking and staying connected with others in your industry can help you stay positive and motivated during your job search.

Attend industry events, join professional groups, and connect with others on LinkedIn. These connections can provide you with support, guidance, and job leads. It's called the silent job market for a reason… Use it to your advantage.

Keep Perspective

Job searching can be a difficult and stressful process, and it's essential to be kind to yourself. Don't beat yourself up over rejection or setbacks.

Life changes, including layoffs, not making it through the final round of interviews, etc., can happen to anyone. Keep in mind that job searching is a learning process, and each experience can help you grow and improve.

Create a Support System

Creating a support system of family, friends, and mentors can help you stay positive and motivated during your job search. Share your goals and challenges.

Managing Your Emotions

Losing a job can be a devastating experience, and it is natural to feel a range of emotions, including sadness, anger, and anxiety. However, it is crucial to allow yourself to go through the grief process and acknowledge your emotions to move forward.

The grief process involves different stages, including denial, anger, bargaining, depression, and acceptance. It is vital to understand that everyone goes through these stages at their own pace, and there is no right or wrong way to grieve. Allow yourself to feel your emotions. Reach out to friends and family for support, and seek professional help, if needed.

Once you have processed your emotions, it is essential to start focusing on the next steps, including finding a new job. During the interview process, it is crucial to manage your emotions and present yourself in a professional and positive manner. Your potential employer will be looking for someone who can handle pressure and manage emotions effectively. Showing you can do so will help you stand out.

Be honest about your previous job loss, but avoid dwelling on it or speaking negatively about your former employer. Instead, focus on what you learned from the experience and how you plan to use that knowledge in your future career. Highlight your strengths, skills, and achievements, and demonstrate your enthusiasm and dedication to the new role.

Remember that the interview process is a two-way street, and you should also be evaluating whether the position and company are a good fit for you. Ask thoughtful questions about the company culture, job responsibilities, and opportunities for growth, and be honest about your expectations and goals.

In summary, going through the grief process after being laid off is essential to process your emotions and move forward. Managing your emotions during the interview process is also crucial in order to present yourself positively and effectively.

By acknowledging your feelings, focusing on your strengths and achievements, and evaluating the fit of the new job and company, you can increase your chances of finding a fulfilling and successful career path.

Thank Those Who Help You Along The Way

Remember to send a thank you to those who help you in your job search, as this is a crucial step in maintaining good relationships and demonstrating gratitude for the time and effort someone has invested in you. Whether it is a family member, friend, or professional contact, taking the time to express your appreciation can help to strengthen the bond you share and pave the way for future interactions.

Not only does a thank you letter show your appreciation, but it can also leave a lasting positive impression on the person who helped you. This can be especially important when it comes to networking and building relationships in your industry. By taking the time to send a personalized thank you letter, you demonstrate that you value the time and expertise of the person who helped you and that you are committed to fostering a positive relationship with them.

Additionally, a thank you letter can help to set you apart from other job seekers who may not have taken the time to show their appreciation. In a competitive job market, any edge you can get can be valuable, and demonstrating your gratitude can help to make you a more attractive candidate to potential employers.

Sending a thank you letter after receiving help in your job search is a small but powerful gesture that can help you to build strong professional relationships, demonstrate your gratitude, and set yourself apart from other job seekers. Whether it's a handwritten note or a thoughtful email, taking the time to say thank you is always a worthwhile investment in your professional future.

Evaluating Your Strengths and Achievements

One of the first steps toward maintaining a positive mindset during the job search is to evaluate your strengths and achievements. Take some time to reflect on your past experiences, education, and skills. Create a list of your accomplishments and what you've learned from each experience. This exercise will help you to recognize your value and potential.

It's essential to acknowledge that not all of your self-worth should be tied to your job or employment status. You are more than your job, and your self-worth should not be determined by external factors. Remember you have strengths and abilities that go beyond your job and that you bring value to the table.

Overcoming Challenges

The job search process can be challenging, and it's essential to recognize that setbacks and rejections are a part of the process. However, it's important to approach these challenges with a positive mindset.

Instead of dwelling on the negative, focus on the positives, and learn from the experience. Use the feedback provided to improve your approach and tailor your applications.

Additionally, it's important to maintain a healthy work-life balance during the job search process. Set achievable goals and take breaks to avoid burnout. Make time for hobbies, exercise, and spending time with loved ones.

Staying Motivated

Staying motivated during the job search process can be a struggle, especially during long periods of unemployment. It's important to remember that just because you aren't where you want to be now doesn't mean you'll never get there. Use this time to develop new skills, take courses, and network with professionals in your field.

Another way to stay motivated is to set achievable goals and break them down into manageable steps. Celebrate small wins along the way, and keep a positive attitude. Remember that your attitude and mindset will determine your success.

Maintaining a positive mindset during the job search process can be challenging, but it's essential to approach the process with a positive attitude. Remember that your mindset will determine the difference between landing and not landing a job.

Take time to evaluate your strengths and achievements, overcome challenges, and stay motivated. Keep in mind that, just because you aren't where you want to be now, it doesn't mean you'll never get there. With the right mindset and approach, you can achieve your career goals.

Ikigai

Ikigai is a Japanese concept that can help people find their purpose in life. It is designed to help those in their journey of self-discovery. Ikigai can serve as a guiding light throughout the job search leading you to your true north.

Ikigai can be translated as "reason for being" or "purpose in life," and it is a combination of four elements: what you love, what you are good at, what the world needs, and what you can be paid for. When you find the intersection of these four elements, you can discover your ikigai and find fulfillment in your life.

One of the key benefits of discovering your ikigai is that it can help you live a more meaningful life. When you have a clear purpose, you can focus your energy and efforts on what matters most to you. You can wake up each day with a sense of excitement and purpose, knowing you are making a difference in the world.

Another benefit of ikigai is that it can help you overcome challenges and obstacles. When you have a strong sense of purpose, you can stay motivated and resilient in the face of adversity. You can draw on your ikigai to give you the strength and courage to keep going, even when things get tough.

Discovering your ikigai is a journey. It requires self-reflection, introspection, and exploration. You may need to try new things, step outside of your comfort zone, and experiment with different activities and pursuits. But the rewards of finding your ikigai are well worth the effort.

I encourage readers to be patient and compassionate with themselves as they embark on this journey. It may take time to find your ikigai, and that's okay. The process of self-discovery is a lifelong one, and each step along the way can bring new insights and revelations.

Discovering your ikigai is a powerful tool for finding purpose and fulfillment in life. It can help you overcome challenges, live a more meaningful life, and make a positive impact on the world. I encourage you all to find your Ikigai today and use it as a tool throughout the job search process.

Quantifying Success = Attitude

Quantifying success is an important aspect of achieving one's goals and objectives. It involves measuring the progress made toward achieving a specific goal or set of goals, and determining whether or not the desired outcomes have been achieved.

Success can be quantified using a variety of metrics, such as financial performance, customer satisfaction, employee engagement, or social impact. However, it's important to note that success is not just about achieving external measures of success. It also comes down to your attitude toward success.

Your mindset, beliefs, and habits play a critical role in determining your success in life. For instance, having a growth mindset, being optimistic, being persistent, and taking calculated risks are all attitudes that can help you achieve success.

In addition, success is not just about achieving external measures of success. It's also about personal growth and fulfillment. It's about aligning your actions with your values, purpose, and passion. This means that success is not just about achieving a certain level of financial wealth or social status. It is also about having a sense of purpose, personal fulfillment, and happiness.

Ultimately, quantifying success requires a combination of external and internal measures. It involves setting specific goals and objectives, tracking progress, and adjusting course when necessary. But it also requires cultivating the right attitude, beliefs, and habits that can help you achieve success in a meaningful and fulfilling way.

You are NOT a failure. It's all about perspective.

It's natural to feel like a failure or to take the job search personally, when you're out of work or struggling to find a new job. However, it's important to remember that your worth as a person is not defined by your employment status or your ability to find a job quickly.

Choosing a positive mindset can make a huge difference in how you approach the job search. Instead of dwelling on negative thoughts or letting rejection get you down, try to focus on the things you're grateful for and the small wins along the way. Celebrate each job application you submit or each interview you land, even if it doesn't result in a job offer.

Remember that the job search is a process, and it often takes time to find the right opportunity. Don't be too hard on yourself if things don't happen as quickly as you'd like them to. Instead, focus on taking action toward your goals, whether that's networking, attending job fairs, or honing your skills.

It's also important to try not to take rejections personally. Remember: there are many factors that go into hiring decisions. A rejection doesn't necessarily mean you're not qualified or not a good fit for a particular role. Try to learn from each experience and use it to improve your approach for future opportunities.

In summary, maintaining a positive mindset during the job search can help you stay motivated, take action toward your goals, and ultimately find the right opportunity for you. Remember that your employment status does not define your worth. It's okay to take some time to find the right fit.

Conclusion

THANK YOU FOR completing this book. We hope you learned something new on effective branding, using a properly formatted resume, and maximizing your LinkedIn profile to help you and your next job opportunity. You may not be in the job market today, but why wait until you are?

Remember: It's easier to cross a bridge that you've already built. You never know when you'll be looking for that next opportunity. Hopefully, you've built and maintained your brand and network so you can leverage it whenever you need it.

Take the steps to make yourself marketable today. Get noticed. Learn something new. Prove your knowledge and get that certificate. That certificate may just be the deciding point between choosing you or the other interviewee.

Remember, *you* are all in sales. *You* are the product. The amount of effort you put into your branding and how big your network are the two factors that will determine if there's an opportunity for you, if you're unemployed, or if there's a better opportunity, if you're currently employed.

If you're interested in group workshops or one-on-one coaching, please use the "Contact Us" button found on our website:

https://www.brandandland.net

Acknowledgments

WE WANT TO THANK all of the folks who've helped or inspired us to create this Recipe for Job Hunting success:

Patt Chowdhury, Rebecca Cooper, Alba Gonzalez, Dave Garrett, Blake Hampton, Marka Hughes, James Jackson, Ramadevi Lanka, Lee Lambert, Mei Lin, Deborah Mangaoang, Alecia McLochlin, Project Management Institute Global, Rene Ramirez, James Reckon, Shoko Sobata, Tammo Wilkens, Iwona Wilson, and all Brand and Land "Live event" attendees and alumni

About the Authors

John Signo, Signofied founder and presenter, is currently a Senior Project Manager at Bank of America, managing Data Management Technology projects with the goal of reducing identified risks while protecting the enterprise and its clients. He has previous work experience at J Walter Thompson, IBM, and BNSF Railway, providing Project Management and Systems Engineering work.

John continues to be an active member of PMI Dallas and PMI Dallas Toastmasters since 2014 and 2015, respectively. He is an advocate for PMI certifications and currently holds the PMI PMP and PMI ACP certifications. In his spare time, he provides sessions on "Branding to Land Your Next Gig" using LinkedIn, resumes, and an online ATS tool. In addition, he continues to mentor PMP and ACP candidates as they prep for their certification exams.

Mohun Sundar, Signofied presenter, has been a member of PMI Dallas since 2013. He is a certified PMP and PMI-ACP and has 10+ years of experience in healthcare project management working with business and IT groups to achieve successful outcomes.

In addition, he has been with PMI Dallas Toastmasters since 2014 and earned his Distinguished Toastmaster certification in 2020. Currently, he works as a senior project manager at Blue Cross Blue Shield of Texas. As part of the Brand and Land team, he looks forward to the opportunity to help others in their journey to improve and optimize their professional brand.

www.ingramcontent.com/pod-product-compliance
Lightning Source LLC
Chambersburg PA
CBHW020448220526
45464CB00002B/916